A collection of extraordinary depth and focus. Powerfully conceived and executed, these poems give complex voice to the multi-stranded miseries and ecstasies of the ghosts of the old Abbotsford convent: the bewildered orphans, left always with a childhood 'that cannot unbandage itself', the wild girls swimming the Yarra to freedom in the shadow of the Skipping Girl; and the nuns, whose sometimes punitive practice co-exists with a creed of love that offers moments of ambiguous radiance 'as if an archangel tapped on your soul'.

—Jennifer Strauss

Spirited and fugitive, lively and resistant, the girls in these poems speak through a powerful blend of the lyrical and the verbatim in a bare, intense, even visionary form of 'writing back' – against and into history. These are moving, compassionate poems full of the motif of river: life, undercurrent, debris – and the deeply aspiring self.

—Philip Salom

Full of resonance and intensity, this collection makes a moving and poetically agile journey through inner voices and voices on record, through memory archives and physical remnants. It offers both a multilayered narrative and a lyric celebration of decades of lives within the walls of an old Melbourne convent. The work is, ultimately, an act of retrieval that is, by turn, luminous, wry, defiant and empathic. Patricia Sykes is a poet who knows not to be constricted by boundaries, who brings into play all the resources of history and reverie, remembrance and vision, in this supple interweaving of lyric intimacy, documentary, liturgy and plain-speaking.

—Jill Jones

It is impossible to read these words – this record – and remain indifferent.

—Kevin Brophy

'How we add up is not how we add up', as Sykes so knowingly and affectingly puts it. This is a volume to both honour and challenge what it is to be abandoned, displaced, institutionalised. True the preconceptions, the cliches and shared common ground are here too, but most strikingly it is the individual and the individual nature of experience that is at once so plainly and poetically expressed. As one who knows intimately the difficulties and complicated pleasures of this particular 'childhood', I can say without reservation – the nail and the hammer, right on the head Patricia!

—Terry Jaensch

In this complex work, Patricia Sykes has chosen a kaleidoscopic technique which has allowed the reader/listener access to the experiential – the personal and specific – while engaging the oblique and suggestive qualities of poetry. She has allowed an entry point to the knotted themes which arise from religious incarceration, positive and negative: bonding, womanhood and spirituality; occultation, exploitation and loneliness. This is an important poetic rendering of a barely known history.

—Anna Kerdijk Nicholson

We hear a polyphony of reminiscent voices stung with pain. More that that, we hear discord tuned to symphony by a poet using the melodics of love. Love not only for the girls who have survived to become confidantes but also for language itself, with its power to undo the curses a cold world can deliver.

—Ross Gibson

The narrative force of Patricia Sykes new collection is astonishing. Each poem is both moving and disturbing, as humble as it is sad. *The Abbotsford Mysteries* manages to be very much *sui generis*, while remaining intensely accessible. I can think of no other recent book in which History and Art get on so well. Definitely a must-read.

—Rob Riel

Patricia Sykes is a poet and librettist. Her poems have won the John Shaw Neilson, Tom Collins, and Newcastle Poetry Prizes. *Wire Dancing*, her first collection of poetry, arose out of her experiences as a performer with the Women's Circus and was commended in the Anne Elder and Mary Gilmore awards. Her second, *Modewarre – home ground*, was shortlisted for the Judith Wright Award. In 2006 she was Asialink writer in residence in Malaysia. Patricia's two collaborations with Australian composer Liza Lim are *Mother Tongue*, a piece for soprano and 15 instruments, and *The Navigator*, a chamber opera, which was nominated in the Green Room and Helpmann awards. Performances of these works include Brisbane Bicentennial Arts Festival, Melbourne International Arts Festival, Huddersfield International Contemporary Music Festival (UK), the Festival d'Automne (Paris), MaerzMusik (Berlin) and the Chekhov Theatre Festival (Moscow).

OTHER WORKS BY PATRICIA SYKES

POETRY

Wire Dancing (Spinifex Press, 1999)

Modewarre: Home ground (Spinifex Press, 2004)

ANTHOLOGIES

Women's Circus: Leaping off the edge (with Deb Lewis, Adrienne Liebmann, Jen Jordan, Louise Radcliffe-Smith, and Jean Taylor. Spinifex Press, 1997)

CHAPBOOK

Performing the Belly (previously published poems. Picaro Press, 2010)

TEXTS FOR MUSIC

Mother Tongue (for soprano and fifteen instruments. Music by Liza Lim, 2005)

The Navigator (opera. Music by Liza Lim, 2008)

The Abbotsford Mysteries

Patricia Sykes

First published by Spinifex Press 2011

Spinifex Press Pty Ltd
504 Queensberry St
North Melbourne, Victoria 3051
Australia
women@spinifexpress.com.au
www.spinifexpress.com.au

Cover design by Deb Snibson, MAPG
Typeset by Claire Warren
Printed by McPherson's Printing Group

National Library of Australia Cataloguing-in-Publication entry

Sykes, Patricia, 1941–
The Abbotsford mysteries / Patricia Sykes.
9781876756956 (pbk)
9781742197678 (ebook: pdf)
9781742197715 (ebook: epub)
Australian poetry—21st century.
A821.4

For my sisters, Elaine, Anni, and Robyn (deceased),
and the Abbotsford 'girls'

Love the girls, love them very much

—St Mary Euphrasia Pelletier

(born Rose Virginie Pelletier, Noirmoutier, France)

Founder and first Superior General of the Sisters of the Good Shepherd

Acknowledgements

The ten poems which make up *the joyfuls* were published in a slightly earlier form in *The honey fills the cone*, the Newcastle Poetry Prize anthology for 2006. My thanks to the judges and the Hunter Writers Centre. Appreciation also to bernie m janssen whose *Tongue-atorium* project at the Abbotsford Convent in 2010 was the perfect context for presenting some of the poems. I am grateful to Arts Victoria for the Development Grant which supported the research and early draft stages of the work. I have drawn from experiences of all three houses, known as 'classes', of the Convent: St Joseph's (the orphanage) St Mary's (for country girls and later for migrant girls) and the Sacred Heart (for 'wayward girls' and older women). My very special thanks to my sisters and the other ex-residents I interviewed, over seventy in all, including nuns and auxiliaries, who were at the Convent for varying periods between the years 1927 and the early 1970s when it ceased to operate as a Catholic institution. Their memories and anecdotes, along with my own, are woven through the poems and I thank them for their trust. Thanks also to Sr Anne Dalton, former province leader, her assistant Kate Graham, and to Fraser Faithfull, archivist to the Good Shepherd Sisters, for their time and patience in dealing with my endless questions. Thanks too to the Abbotsford Foundation for the use of a studio for six months in 2005/2006, and for its interest and support for the project, especially Katherine McLean, Marie-Claire Courtin, Sally Romanes, Tony

Lee and Nigel Lewis. It is a rare privilege to be able to return to a childhood institution after it has begun a new life as an arts precinct. I am indebted to poet Jordie Albiston for her careful reading of the manuscript and her perceptive editing. The title of the poem 'Death's Dream Kingdom' owes its origin to 'The Hollow Men' by T. S. Eliot. Some of the anecdotal material in the poem 'Edified' is taken from *Built Upon a Hilltop. A History of the Good Shepherd Sisters in Western Australia 1902–2002* and I thank the author, Geraldine Byrne, and the Good Shepherd Sisters of Western Australia for permission to reproduce it. I would also like to acknowledge the importance to my research of *Pitch Your Tents On Distant Shores. A History of the Sisters of the Good Shepherd in Australia, Aotearoa/New Zealand and Tahiti* by Catherine Kovesi. Thanks to Deb Snibson for the cover design and to Claire Warren for her typesetting. My gratitude to all at Spinifex Press, especially Susan Hawthorne and Renate Klein who keep extending their capacity for publishing.

Contents

The Sorrowfuls

The Joyfuls

The Glorious

Rosarium

They seem to have died . . . their going from us

(Wisdom 3: 1-9)

Death's dream kingdom

As sudden as that. A breath taken. Then not.
Then steps. A travel. To place the orphans.
In the capital. Melbourne. New city of
displacement. *Poor kids, you poor kids.*
Her voice all echo. All the-sun-has-set.
In her wake, trails of earth. Droppings from
her torn roots. Goodbye her final scent:
septicaemic stillbirth, caramelised orange
skins. Her womb and the oven now cold as
tombs. Only a fool would worship death's
dream kingdom. Surely only a fool. Her
death is no dream. She will not awaken.

Mutter song

You're going and that's that!   to live
among holy pictures statues rosary beads
with the blue virgin whose son's heart
is not flesh but icon   shining out of his
ribcage like a still-life   a red apple
not for the eating but ever ripe   as if
immortality lives there   the riddle of
sacred pulse forever stopped but never
dead   *it's not fair*   a child crying
(she'll be trouble that one) her outrage
for the human loss just buried in the
earth's dark box   *life goes on*
heart-*torn* heart-*heavy* heart-*scared*

Onus

Thirteen   a tricky number   thirteen months
between oldest, second oldest   seven years
between second oldest and next   a God
number   the tick   day of rest   creation
complete though not perfect   five other
siblings dying at birth, or near to   thirteen
months more between third daughter and last
(did she plan it, the thirteens? lucky, unlucky
the odd always *odd*)   the onus on ten and
nine to mother two and one because *in*
there a precinct of words ending in *shun*
separa*shun*   isola*shun*   aliena*shun*
it wasn't encouraged to be close to your
sisters   prayer, blackboard, job, ahead
of the two in cots   their infancy fluent
in the heart's dumb loss   *the hands in*
the nursery were as the touch of wood
ten, nine, two, one   *hold*   *hold as one*

There will be a girl who

The vertigo of fright has no hidey-hole
we are fear girls now   grief daughters
(we cannot gainsay)   we fear the high
walls   we fear the iron window bars
should we fear the shepherded girls?
come out come out wherever you are
there will be a girl who daydreams
about *owning her own orchestra*
there will be a girl who *wins sixpence*
for dancing the best of all the orphans
in front of the Queen!   at the MCG!
there will be a girl who waits and waits
on *Visiting Sundays* for a father who does
not come (he choofed off *chug chug*) but
he always appears *in November for the*
Melbourne Cup (yeah!) and there will
be a girl who fights another girl, one of
them white (me) the other one black (her)
because they want a scrap and each other will
do so they punch and flail and hit and miss
and leave it at that   though the black girl
will fight on   for rights   hers indigenous
and it will all come true   all of it   true

This viper her tongue

Saying what it wants to say   stinging
where it wants to sting   *all that language*
of love and gentleness   I had a perception
of incredible hypocrisy   tongue whose two
birthdays will grow to years inside the walls
whose sister, oldest, a pale migraine girl, will
escape duty in the sewing room and slip away
to the attic to roll among the clothes up there
as if empty frocks provide hours of warm touch
a bliss of the kindest   not substitute but real
like the cloth she remembers as a second skin
the one that tore itself open in birthing her, that
warmth, that one, whose dead life is the pale girl's
make-believe   a small girl's joy   whose game
is more a rule not to torture her with hope

Providence

All for thee my Lord O my Jesus all for thee
a grandmother of belief, firm beseecher of
providence, *its divine care and ministration*
grandmother whose faith blesses faith's
transformations   her granddaughters in
proof   child brides in white   white frocks-
veils-socks   their white missals ashine with
imitation mother-of-pearl   girls in a tremble
of grace-pride-goodness   the sacred host
dissolving on their tongues   (as it is meant
to)   promised now for life   *let no man*
put asunder   capable now of sin-guilt-
doubt   grandmother whose luscious treats
will arrive as reprieve laced with prayer
some of the convent food so awful it
would turn the stomach of a picture book
grandmother who had her own hotline to the
Mother Superior   then turnabout   the Mother
Superior in retirement (*still a mad poet at 93*)
beseeching the grandmother's grown orphans
for God's sake come visit!   *there's nothing*
to do here but play cards with old women

Panic bell

O that bell that panic that every *Sunday*
that chime that toll that ding-a-dong time's up
that command that bidding that nowhere (no
place) to hide O   *time-to-go time-to time-o*
her home her hold a workaday of long hours
too long and no-one to mind her   the Europe
of family too poor too far   *O damn oh hell*
her nightmares pitched to the sound of bells
for years the *five o'clock summons* a cannon
in her ears a judder in her nerves (*it is hard
to forget*) O yes unless (until) every bell dies

How will you know who you are

If you are unremembered, anonymous
a twerp, an alibi, a refugee, an etcetera
Mother-of-Names wanted me to change
my name because there were too many
Marys   Mary still, Mary always, Mary
in a time of no names   *so the Jewish*
girls could be infiltrated among us   kept
hidden   their numbers tattooed on their
skins   ours tattooed on our clothes, in
our chants   *twenty-two, who are you?*
in a time of disguise   in a time of
forgetting   remember your name
remember your rhyme   remember
how   and how   to find yourself

Gamble

O parent of the rod and the threat (*if*
you don't behave you are going back!)
are you the same infectious laugh
who teaches me to sing in harmony
and how to use mind-reading tricks
to spot the ace lurking up your sleeve
O parent are you the thin-lipped scowl
that parks us outside the walls   our
suitcases expectant   letting us sweat
and tremble until you relent   (*I used to*
think the convent was where the unlove-
able kids went) this third time we might
call your bluff   take our cases and
walk   never fully to come back

Creed

I believe I believe in Skipping Girl Vinegar *my guardian dear ever this night be at my side, to light and guard, to guard and guide* my Angel-of-Neon my skipping rope wings her factory rooftop my heaven (*my destiny-heaven*) *seek and ye shall find*
I believe in my feet flying again like hers smiling, highing, never a stumble, never a skip missed by day by night soaring higher than death, higher than the exile that follows death (the shutting behind walls *for the good of*) I believe in the day that will come I believe in the rope that is wings I believe in the beckoning light I believe in my feet on the road in skippety-skip beats yes yes my freed feet

Gloria

How many roses make a family?
The garden a split trinity *snip*
snip as if secateurs are busy
against cross-contamination
St Josephs for the orphans
St Marys for the medley girls
Sacred Heart for the waywards
we never associated, we had our
home they had theirs yet *Gloria*
Gloria our perfume is everywhere

The Luminous

It's not how long I was there
It's been part of my life

Rose, roses, rosary

Beginning with a great idea
Rose Virginie saying *come*
the roses that were dying

beginning to open in a loop of
hands, a prayer-string of nuns
who birth daughters uniquely

'we the mothers, you the child
whether your age is three or
ninety-three   it is *the system*'

a replica, down the centuries,
of *holy family*, a faith ideal
a myste among the mysteries

the bewildered foetal ones
listening for the heart sound
the source   the nuns com-

pressed like petals between
lay and religious, diocese and
state, the multiple birthings,

and their own vocation
it was unnatural   it made
them frustrated   made them

our morning and evening star
torn between God's red force
and the Virgin's blue peace

between the life of spirit and the
practicals of governance, bidden
and held among thorns of the fold

Miasmata

Birrarung, *river of mists and shadows*
drifts of white in a dark hover
as if breath here grew inconsolable

this was the Abbotsford property
the name of which has now become
so celebrated

big praise for the trouble-girls gifted by
the poor, the dead, the drunk, the mad

keep your eyes down or you'll become like them
like the women gifted by fear or fault
some desperate enough to gift themselves

or like the nuns, offering themselves
by relative choice, the sweet debris
of drenched lives, drowning or afloat
the river as red aorta   believe

how the wanderings of water
stress the imprisoned pulse
I became afraid for my own heart
believe the river when it says *amen*

Coils

As if women are rivers
as if they must be kept
from deviating like this Yarra

river from which *a severe loop*
was eliminated, always someone
searching its banks

for a daughter they once misplaced
though the only fontanelles now
are history's, river grasses, weeds

pigeons roosting the bridge mess the signs
but old tracks know their own
footprints   first the Kulin women's

food and infants on their backs
their naked feet gripping the rocks
against the water's rush

upstream, downstream, their scent
all over it, then our own, convent
women and kids strung together

like a rosary, like a chain
against flood, debris, drought
ave, ave, like a faith in a river

The door

It used to seem so big

as it loomed, opened, shut,
a doom approaching dead weight,
the way a tomb shuts off all light

the numb entry worse in the day
worst at night, instantly captive
to the door's metal plate, its scrape

and slide, its scrutinising eyes
no exit visa to the outside
nothing but a strange new

cacophony of beds, baths,
tables, chairs, so many voices
tossing among storms, girl

now subject to alien rules
and whatever dark fears enter
if she opens too wide

true partnership can only be achieved
by separate and whole beings
someone here speaking as Gebo,

the rune, of the spirit
which is internal and resists
I wasn't going to let them break me

Iambic pentameter

I watch myself   how I use my voice   how
much I give away   rebellion weighs
against obedience   prayer against fantasy
rote against the thrill of words that lately arrive

It was hearing a girl recite Ode to a Cabbage
that made me want to write verse myself
I hide my poems like hoarded love
the taste of secrecy is delicious (*Nun-*

the-Big-Irish gives the girl curry
when she catches her kissing my cheek)
now Mother-of-the-Blackboard
proving with chalk that poetry has feet

˘ / ˘ / ˘ / ˘ / ˘ /

If a thing is not prayer why must it be sacrilege?
We are children of rhythm as well as of God
I am learning body worship from *a girl who*
walks beautifully   where else but here

could I rejoice such things?   Father,
are you listening? I'm your little exile no more
You would not know me   I am metric now
My feet are my own   how you will miss me

Each phantom ache an amputee

In the whisper trenches
counting parents, siblings
the way you audit fingers and toes
like confetti you're all scattered everywhere

the Museum-of-the-Lost a camouflage of files
a shuffler of mingle dusts
I was determined never to marry an Australian
in case I married my brother

skin memory's lifetime touch
who can cut you as utterly
as the one who holds the sword?
our guardian was a mongrel, he split us up

the razor of power having such adult force
in a time of apologies the authorities aghast
and the era that meant it for the best
put to bed as history

nothing will ever be as bad
day, night, the seasons, the search
each year on her birthday
the ex Ward-of-State

who advertises in periodicals of hope
unable yet to strew rose petals
for a mother unearthed *I asked my father*
you didn't kill her did you? I might've, he said

The man in the moon and the axe of God

WELCOME THE CHILD, AROUND WHOM EVERYTHING

Tabernacle — this child learning to
cuddle hope and smirk at fate is curious
to know how each day your mouth
can so cleanly devour and disgorge God

ANNOUNCE YOUR MYSTERY AND SAY YOUR PRAYER

Mystery — the man in the moon
wielding the axe of God
like a Viking

Prayer — my aim in life is clemency

ALL GOD'S SERVANTS ARE EQUAL

but if-when the axe falls only one neck
will be first   we grow old in prayer
Catholic knees are among the old-age
diseases that beset us   we grow edgy

among flicker breaths   the candles
check us for piety   they count our
prayers but will not say if they kneel
to the axe or a Jesus on the tease

the axe so tuned to *perditio* we should quail

between blessing and curse
between penance and grace
between salvation and not

I got slapped for asking
what a womb was, as in
blessed is thy womb

Tabernacle — as if you are
too pure for our mouths?

Bloodline

Holy Mothers

are all your wombs virgins?
The question is a red line
that must not be crossed
or it might bleed copiously
like the spear in the side
of the Jesus whose blood
must be drunk to keep him alive.

Holy Mothers

how can it be wicked
to hold that women and girls
are true sufferers of blood?
The blood all over the toilet walls
is the blood of menstruating girls

(I couldn't believe birth
came out of such a dirty place).

Holy Mothers

some of us know, have felt,
the agony of bringing forth
from the warm taboo that bore

the holy infant   what are we to
name it if not womb? *Lifeline?*
Shipwreck? O birth and death.

Institutional

How we add up is not how we add up.
A woman who *blames her mother,*
not God, wanted badly *to kill her.*

A woman who adores hers admires
the discipline of inherent character
her mother learnt from the nuns (*yes*

and but, the *inherent* is dependent)
and how this led to a tolerance, her
daughter at seventeen reading Marx

(*yes and but,* she had access) and if *dis-*
placement is the big theme for all of us
why do some of us never leave while

some who have left fight a longing to
return. (*Yes and but,* what other home is
so *theirs*). What has deportment to do

with it? Mothers, you hold up *how a cat*
moves, its grace, its sinuous elegance
but have you questioned the nature of

homage? Have you imagined (or is the
system too storial, too set) a convent
of priests, boy orphans, wayward men,

on their knees to a female God and
hierarchy of priestesses? (*yes and but*)
How we add up is not how we add up.

Architecture

The *nature* of the place
revealing itself to us
as a troubled blueprint

we wander like the bewildered
who have lost everything
and return to find it still here

the years we buried behind
grey mince-meat walls
still present in the faces

which are not our faces
who trail us like the ghosts
of unfinished things   the best

the worst   the unspeakable
we were a smorgasbord
for paedophiles

heads nod   heads shake   truth
as difficult to prove as differing
histories   *even so even so*

a haunt of eyes asking how
can you trust the sound that is not
a butterfly sucking on nectar

Gloria

Kyrie eleison
our voices shiver
above the narthex
if we could dance
our blood would warm
us   *Lord O Lord*
we're hivey-jive girls
rock'n'roll girls (we
keep your picture next
to Elvis) *Kyrie eleison*

The Sorrowfuls

As I lay me down to sleep

Aspect

The view through the bars to the bridge the cars
the winding disappearance
of speeding roads

out there my ghost self
on legs long and fleeing from the sanctioned care
that feeds the door with young

all the live ones   vanishing
to the houses of Mary   Joseph   Magdalen
tonight another cry among the wheels
an infant in a shawl

placed by her mother

a doorstep dump in the dark   a call on
compassion   left to the wind she'd be a leaf
a rag   the beat of a quaver   quickly blown

we'd have been on the streets
if it weren't for the nuns

O street where I lived
are you as dead as they say? wouldn't I rather
be Magdalen than saint?
O fear is it you
keeping me gaoled   (is it true?)   so I won't
chase a ghost self down a dead-end street?

Lent

The ritual cross on our foreheads
burning like submission

the dead too in their ashen skins
unable to escape God's coffin

we had to file past the bodies in the church
they'd put a net over the coffins
I hated it, I can still smell
the embalming

sleep is not peace it is night's infection
the lights flashing on the bridge
are the eyes of dead nuns

impossibly they rise with the moon
does vigilance never die?

the Holy Mothers keep hunting redemption
in us   in everyone   in the Ronald Ryan
who is due to be hanged   giving sanctuary

(*the whisper says*) to his mother
while the appeal is on   hiding her away
from the busybody press

we had to go to mass more often
say more rosaries
I became so impatient

the ritual cross a true cross
O sad noose   O burden   O testing

Deadly endings

The new girl walks like an accident
once she was safe in a dream
of riding pillion until

the priest who rides the Vespa
placed the host upon her tongue
and her half-petticoat fell down

no not *call call the mocking bird*
no not wishing to peck at her
she is teaching us what to fear

I was fourteen
that thing who married my father
put me in the orphanage
for a virginity test

we can tell she is innocent
by the way shame strips her
naked   by the guilt
she calls love-wishing

all I ever wanted
was someone to love me

the walls such bad lovers   holding
her for years in their cold stone crush

such a hard hard hold she turns
and returns to a passionate embrace

I used to fantasise all the time
it continued for years and years
I'd fall madly in love with someone
then they'd die   my fantasies
always had deadly endings

Persecuting colour

How now brown cow!

the brown woman carries on sweeping
here since infancy wouldn't you think
she'd be suffering

but no *she's a big noise*
she has clout with the nuns

the swept ground also brown
shadows moving over it
like years passing

everything I wanted and got
brought trouble to me

my haunted sister
fearing the woman is contagious

a brownness she attracts
and cannot outrun

how now brown cow!

the ridicule   her fear
the dust hardening her tongue

PUC SUX

An overnight graffito
wearing the sheen of fresh blood

suspicion is pointing its hunting finger
it was not us in the night
who crept out and blasphemed on the walls

—it is safest to be anonymous
punishment falls hardest on obvious backs
my twin says like ours

our red hair, our singing, our talking to a man

if we are wicked we cannot be scarce?

the St Joseph's girls threatened
with being sent to the Sacred Heart
the Sacred Heart girls threatened
with being sent to Fairlea

(praise God our mother recovered
from the mental hospital)

benedictio your indulgences
keep slipping through our fingers

why do you fall at all
if you fall so far from our unbowed heads?

O benedictio how many *ex-Abbotsford girls*
go on to be hoarders?

we must learn
to bless ourselves we must plan I plan
to nurse among clutters of the unforgiven

Mortal, venial

In the humid confessional
everything is epic

I didn't like the priests
they'd come from the seminary
one used to ask sex questions
he wanted to know if I had sex with a dog
I was shaking, I never heard anything like it
I came out and said Hail Mary after Hail Mary

during the penance hour
my sins fly off
like freed doves

isn't sin beautiful in flight?

I swore three times
I stole apples from the pig bucket
I accuse myself of accusing myself

God will steal your brains off you
it's Mother Vigilance
in joking shoes

I want to tell and tell
about the priest's sex dog

but *mea culpa* I'm no tell-tale tit

and who would take my word
against a priest's? so *mea culpa*

I'm keeping it hid   in a hole
in the ground   my soul
in the hole   my shame pit

Bad girls do the best sheets

In our hands grey becomes white
white becomes income   our skin rubbed
to raw is nothing that women out there
are not enduring or loathing

don't complain   say three Hail Marys

except where is the balm
in the scrubbing and tending
of linen in whose bed
you will never be permitted

I don't think God listened
to my prayers in those days

we launder and sort, inventories of *perhaps, never*

for god's sake it was staffed by children
It bloody cleans it up
to say it was a commercial laundry

cleanliness next to Godliness is not always
spotless   some of our trough-dreams ending
as scurf   some popping like soap bubbles
a few living long enough to dodge the Bishop's

Parlour

(the privilege room
you only passed through
when you arrived or left)

and barter with the drivers *swapping sex*
for a getaway ride the jiggity-jig laundry vans
as golden coach going all the way

Mellifer

Mellifer, mellifluous   girl biding
her time among petals, thorns
the sheen and prick of dutiful wounds

I swam across the Yarra
and got myself pregnant
so I couldn't be sent back

on the Pomegranate Path a visitor
in the aftermath praising the garden
the fruit   *oh she's rough as bags*
a Dismissive says

Mellifer, mellifluous
girl of fraught strokes   fatigued
and aglitter with the river's wet kiss
'a tainted Eve'   (*sticks and stones!*)

I'll go to God my own way thanks

who bears her ruby seeds
among unloving streets   matched by
the stories she hears   her own
giving back

I ate, I relished, I shared it around

Mellifer, mellifluous
honey-bearer who refuses
to offer up her foetus as tithe

Honorary

It was good to meet the girl who swam the Yarra

honour rolls not kept of the runaways
the fled ripples of their bodies, lives
the snags the currents the muddy holes
that could have reached up and taken them

the medals exclusive to *Children of Mary* girls
their glitter and wink and pious brag
did you ever and only wish you had one?

you had to kneel
and say please Mother
do you think I am worthy?
the answer I got was always a no

and torment has not forgotten the foliage girls
how they climbed and clung like scrambler
monkeys   heroines of their own disaster

they were hosed out of the trees
they spent days in the Infirmary

still, what fun we had in the days of the pool

(except the bad girls
never allowed in the pool
with the good)

the licence the play the friendly water

still, whenever I look there's a girl in a tree
falling and felled by water as brutal
as teeth at the throat

still, still, *you either get bitter or better*

Hell, memory

Her ex-child life how it survives
(she is fierce about this)
as evidence of fire

I was a beautiful little girl
they turned me into a monster
four nuns thrashed and flogged me at once
they flogged a little girl to death in front of me
she bit her tongue in half
there was blood everywhere

she's mad! does it gladden her
to watch scepticism dancing on coals?

I'm not vindictive
I just want the truth to come out

how much *does* she know,
could she tell, that girl in a frock with her
hopscotch taw and skipping-rope chant

it was a cruel place
there was a lovelessness

and a childhood *(it is gone)*
that cannot unbandage itself hell

memory, memory, hell   two mad fires
and a burnt child

she will recover

she will not recover

ah the beautiful girl, the pity of it, the pity

Gloria

Give us this day
a stained glass window
our lives etched in it
in dedicatio
and give us this day
creation's full sunlight
to pour our colour
forth over among
the saints and angelics
O give us this day

The Joyfuls

Angelus! Angelus!
The noon bells full of angels

Incarnate

Small days wish the sun away
small days wish the signs
were less luminous less ominous

this is my daughter in whom I am well pleased
this is my womb and she is immaculate

small days are children of doubt
on the roadway where rabbits thrive
un-stunned by the floodlight

of annunciation   small days
say Gabriel was merely delivering sperm
in a bottle, was a trickster like Hermes his

father   they say the incarnation was monstrous
say Mary yeasty and conceived was
merciless, a perfect incubation, behaved

as she should, never perfidious, brought herself
to bear, on time, gave joyous birth, nursed
humbly, tenderly, was wracked only

by the worst   a virgin tested   who
made purity a pinnacle   a woman apart
as though it were simple to withstand divinity

Conceived

It was done unto me   it was
God   Father Son and Holy Ghost

it was my body   living monstrance
for delivering glory

it was me   how is it possible
to live

without *fruit of thy womb*

> *I didn't know the difference*
> *between girls and boys*
> *everybody was just an Australian*
>
> *don't sit on the grass with a man*
> *the nuns said   I was never*
>
> *a good judge of men*
> *we weren't told enough*

in a time of aprons one thing hides another
the grass grows strangely conceptive

looking over the shoulder is profoundly
ridiculous, green children are all around

those born of ignorance are either loved
or unloved
hail Mary that the womb
grows too old to bear

our own convent mothers
have chosen the erotic distance of God

this next year I can spirit myself anywhere

Bound

Centuries of tenderness and the death kiss
the beginning the end in the lap of cloth

the blankets the shrouds the balms the touch
the hands
you allow and those you are powerless
to stop

you had to kneel by your bed
and get dressed and undressed
under your flannelette nightgown

when we had a bath
you had to wear a cotton bath robe
you weren't allowed to look at your body

our chastity cools the water
we emerge wearing the chill of statues

in shiver-sympathy with dead Mary
her virginity fused to cloth-of-stone white
with a small warm allowance of blue

my own mother a Mary unwrapped
whose name did not begin

with m, which does not signify loss
since her breasts make the shape

of an m, where Magdalen suckled
until she too became an m

Immanent

Atmosphere matters, the flowers
the candles, the priest's gorgeous

robes   the probing incense
permits no privacy   the nerves

could be ours   it could be us
before the nuptial altar of God

is held breath prayer?

(it is only ecstasy) each wondrous dress
stands for beauty   the white novices

converting to darker nuns
(it is only practical)
the satin the lace
whipped away like a froth of the heart

this is what we plucked the chickens
for   gutted and headless they dangle

from tables like those upon which
the white banquet will be placed

during this one hour not even an axe
can behead our immanence

Abiding

Some things abide longest
memory twines itself around favourites

like the sacred brides   *it was soul*
it was virtue   *it was joyful surrender*

it was the quiver of a galaxy
                    the moon in your lap
the tides at your beck
                    something big like that
except the Magdalen smile
                trails a scorpion tail
                                sting
                                sting
each decadent minute of fantastic pain
cutting clear through the ultra

    and the shredding and the shedding
    for the bedding

    and fleas that flee to the high Pyrenees

so attend the virgin beds   as if how otherwise
can you fumigate an escape to high flights?

but Magdalen Elocution have you also
pulled off the enormous   the Milky Way

back in its own dark sheets

and

this is my daughter
in whom I am well pleased

Feast

The aromas of the feast oozing through
the stone-dense walls
                    the laundry Magdalens
craving more
than the specially appointed rest by
grace of the vows grace of the blest

I used to think of putting my hand
through the mangle
so I could get out of here

give *share* we are schooled to this
our share is hungry
it wants to partake of the delicious
laid out for the professed the worshipful

(presentation requires grandeur
grandeur requires worth

in requiring to be fed
we drool like old Magdalens
over the nuns' white noise

the world stops when I hear them
the sound keeps everything intact
it comes in in waves

because of its gentleness
I can float out and meet it

that music those voices
everything in me wants to sing

Fount

There's a nun who cries out to the white peace of faith
she is heard inside the stone fount   deep well where
she hid an old voice   one who was cured by the
waters, who rose from her sickbed, who fulfilled
her pledge to convert from Judaic to Catholic
a switch prayer from side to side tossing

already it is understood she is one of the lost
(who rescues the lost)

when I came here from the Ukraine
through the German refugee camps
I didn't have a word of English
the mother spoke some German
she'd take me by the hand and walk me
round and round the schoolyard at playtime
schulhof   schoolyard   that's how I learnt

we give ourselves to what we need   the ones
who hold back never arrive but how can we tell
what the lost one most needed   she is seen
in the churches in civilian dress   she is heard
in the music of her brilliant hands

the church organs that come alive for her
refuse to sing when she departs

often like a fugitive   a flick of fabric   a
quick dash   it is to be expected   when the
dead walk abroad they are not as we loved them

Edified

It is given that we are children

the poor child had a most violent temper
and was like a wild beast sometimes when in drink

it is given that a woman-child tortures patience

this is my hole
the cupboard where I was punished

the solitary dark of confinement is a nun's anger cooling

early in the year the poor child came home
it was the beginning of the end

the death-bed priest was *edified by her*

she edified her companions by her grand acts of love

she edified the candles whose forgiveness is exquisite
even at her most sinful the wick of grace alight in her

Discipled

From warm yellow roses to the barricades of prayer
I entered as a child   a woman   older   younger

the wayward ones remind me we're the same
the fit of skin bites deeper than appearances

we talk often of gratitude   how they've never known
the equivalent of their now-free underwear

or the luxury of a once-weekly change
I tell them this when their sullenness threatens the collars

under their irons   intimacy binds us like a shroud
this is proved in our renewals   each sloughed cell dies

as a stain   when I teach the children their limerick lace
I remind them how each small pinprick is as nothing

to the Jesus sacrifice   we are lucky to have such a one
a disciple to goodness who catches us as we drain away

Clots

Tenth prayers seal a decade
we begin with this   we end with that

I have heard a Magdalen give thanks
for her enlarged heart

for years I didn't realise
you could choose how you live

on the most joyful days we hurry through
the tenth aves because each tenth one

could be the last   the optimal   the nth
I who was a defect am now a perfect

except the joyfuls never last   mysteriums
of fall and rise huddled together in clots

Mary keeps all these things in her heart
wisdom is astonished at her doctoring

how her name in the beads is the life
of her son   given into our hands

Gloria

From the walls'
four corners
our spent breaths
coming home
to our mouths
our lungs
a canticum
whose voice
is memory
rejoicing

The Glorious

It is a mystery

Crux

I fell in love with purple there.
And shimmer threads. Bathed in light,
the high mass, music, flowers, incense.
No dirt in sight: *pure, purely, purified.*
The robed priests' day selves beautified
as if *halo* shone out of a holy picture
and pulsed in them, and I entranced with
the prayerful sway of a new word, *robe.*

I was a Godly child.
I ate with the nuns and slept with the nuns.

I used to sew the gems onto the silk.
Some of the gowns went to Rome for the Pope.

The nuns used to tell me, in years to come
think how proud you'll be.

If you knew my home life
rotten like my teeth
until I could spell broken.

Everything was made by hand.

The Hand, its A to Z uses.

My hand.

Their hands.

The nuns
sewing me back to myself.
Fabric, scissors, thread.
The stitch of my substance.
The eye of my own needle.
Its jab is all my blood.
This thrives me. This is fact.
This pattern. I make. I live.

God's star

Being there was like acting,
a pretend life   *the real one going on*
without you   *beyond the walls*

I was a Roman Centurion   I placed my
hand on the shoulder of the girl playing
St Dorothea and said *Maid, the snow is*
on the bough   *renounce Christianity O*
renounce   *save yourself from the lions!*

I could have played Caesar
too, *Hail Caesar, those who are about to die*
salute you! But not *The Mikado in a yellow*
kimono, red hair, freckles and a crown.

And not *The Good Ship Lollipop*   the girl
who wanted the role mocked my audition
and stole the song

(though she would not, any more than I,
have been able carry to off the *Liberace*
impersonation).

Can a girl be a dissident, or just
disobedient?   The song stealer ran   came
back in a police car   ran again   as if she

knew small galaxies are swallowed by
larger ones   as if saying *no thanks*
to becoming God's star.

Crocodile file

Our docility is a crocodile.
The garden walks unleash the
hunger in us. The nuns ration
them to control our greed
children are natural gluttons.

Today none of us are widgees
our wild appetites hushed
as if the influence of Retreat
works against the plotting
of something illicit.

Once, the Jesus gardener
told us *he was planting fishes*
he showed us green tails
sticking up out of the ground
they turned out to be onions.

We must have been so innocent. The
squealing is coming from the pigs.
Our crocodile freedom infuriates them.
Their cage day, which is every day,
matches the boil on my leg.

It is envy   the pigs envy our
hormones   our ripe euphoria

(at night some of the girls creep
into other beds for a fondle).
It is not only the pigs   cows

within range of our aura
keep trying to mount each other
as if there's a height they can reach
what are they doing, Mother
what are they doing?

(Our laughter is a metronome.
Mother-of-Piano-Accordion
playing louder and faster, fingers
flinching and flying as if trying
to distract the cows with a jig.)

Visitation of sweetness

Salvation frowns. The holy month keeps slipping
off our shoulders. We're becoming more carnal
afraid joy will be plucked from us with our cloaks.

We had crushes on the Retreat priests.
We'd rush into the cloakroom
and jabber among the coats
then go out and be saintly again.

Is there a patron saint of joy?

Obedience may be the daughter of God
but she knows how to start the whisper
of a rare cake, posted, a gift
a slow delicious crumbling

as if the Retreat priests are an icing
as if this is what transforms
our prayers into intoxicated bees
flying above the chapel roof

through the cakeless spheres
thence to Mary thence to God
humbly from the refreshed
honey of our tongues.

The perfect deception of night

Our thoughts dread night, the silence.
God sees all, hears all, knows all.
What if he eavesdrops, what if he
pries? One of us has spied out the
loose brick that hides the gate key

one frets she'll be *fertile as a box*
of manure (like her mother) and
bear a child like the nuns' *Angel*
of Light   *who sometimes in her*
confusion tries to strangle us. One

is stirred by the dancing, girl with
girl, for an hour on Sundays, *it's a*
wonder we didn't all turn out to be
lesbians. They were more advanced
more streetwise than a lot of us.

Mother-of-the-Dorm your tiny cell
is big with secrets. Do they gnaw
at God? We burn to see the *dowry*
you brought from Ireland or France.
We burn to know who you are under

your nun clothes. We can hear water
and cloth. We guess at nakedness

and baldness yet each morning
you reappear as if you had slept
not in your bed but in your habit

and nothing creased or missing
betrays whether you spent the hours
shut from us in vision or nightmare.
Except today your brass key,
our pitiless morning call, rings

against the door jamb like a *jubilate*
and you are wearing radiance, as if
an archangel tapped on your soul
and said *you are chosen*   as if
nothing we do after can shatter this.

Winged ascent

We learn it on humility knees.
A Holy Ascent requires a God
a throne a cloud of glory.
Jubilation too is on the list
triumph and wounds
                    especially
you need to be pierced
in the hands, the feet, the full stigmata

we used to cut our knees with lemonade bottles
so we wouldn't have to go to mass.
It didn't work. It didn't make the blood pour.

What does red devilry care
for glass knife and surface pain?
I pretended I flew into the great gate once
the Infirmary knowing always
if you are faking or truly concussed

one girl had a fit and died. She was mentally disabled.
The Infirmary let go some white doves in honour of her.
We were told it was her soul going to heaven.

My small sister then
building a worry of doves
a fret about black and white

the nuns' habits flup-flupping
in the flyaway wind inflaming
her fear of crows. The noises
coming from her mouth only sound
like words. I know they're a crying.
She wants the winged soul back.
And the flying and the soaring.
The beautiful ascent that never dies.

Glass story

As if we fit together like old shards
orphan, unfortunate, drunk, prostitute
in a neat history of broken glass

like exotics for the curious
who've come awkward with pity
to view life behind the walls

we could tell them a thing or two

or three   an ex-Magdalen
of transparent impatience
wanting only answers   *why*

do women let themselves
suffer so damn much!
                              logic, she says
(an ex-Magdalen
of transparent impatience
wants *only* answers

why do women let themselves
suffer so damn much!)
                              logic, she says
relieves the mind, while exorcism
frees the emotions, closer

to her theory of how after an event
the rational is at best a shovel
her laugh is speculative

what to unearth, how much,
how many windows
she could break in the telling

when I tell him what happened
my husband says those things didn't happen
you'd better not say things like that
what might people think?

Beloved

One by one we are dying off.

Things move on. Gratitude
for what is left is not only
for what is curled up and warm.

Years adore whatever there is to lose
a foot still dancing or limping
a tooth still eating or decaying

any life that moves
along any road that is willing.
Do you have a pocket saved

that has a shilling to spend?
Any gone currency with a tongue
to name and prolong itself

the way *this is my beloved*
kept spending itself
in our orphan prayers?

How we became borne
became light itself, flew,
uplifting each thing we touched

because we were joyous
because we trusted it
because no walls could hold us.

Having lost all fear

The Holy Mothers sustain our desert
their days and nights
of exertion keeping us alive
a sweat so copious the priestly laws
are confounded, the skill meant to be
a Jesus one, proof of a miracle,
a big fountain. Each day's water
continues to be necessary.
Rebels or not we visit the oasis.
Religious or not we drink
what will change us.
The church would never
allow it. Its hierarchy
continues to deify itself.
Having lost all fear
the nuns carry on
a loving disobedience
(they know church men
are also as children)
while on a table-top of sand
a needle keeps working
a beautiful big supper cloth
with poinsettias all over it
the miracle of becoming
a garden where there was none

so that when the last supper
comes around again
we are certain to be flowers.

Trusting the donkey

Awaiting the donkey who bears destiny towards straw.
In summer we used to tease the new horsehair for the mattresses. We'd do a different dormitory each year.
From our lumpy beds we scan the stars. None grow
larger, brighter. Can the story have written itself wrong?
Hospitality has shut its doors. The refectory is dishing up
potato rot, weevils. And for how long can the cockroaches
keep tonight awake? Our nightgown prayers cannot hold
their wide eyes open. *I'd dream myself onto a small boat then perch myself over the side and go to the toilet.*
The morning tide rides high in the drenched bed. The holy
infant is hidden among the crib's stone faces. And on the
cold righteous floor a rebuked child kneels hour-long under
her cold wet sheet. Yet when the bells peal we breathe as
one with the donkey and sing the born sky's pale rose.
And surely the blood in the straw blesses us with love.
And surely we are some way on some ladder to saved.

Gloria

Mater Assumptio
The blessed rose
dying out of World
into Eternity   not
canker not gall rot
not withering plague
The rain not at fault
The sun warmly kind
It is not the elements
It is written

Other Titles by Patricia Sykes

Modewarre: Home Ground

Shortlisted, Judith Wright Award, 2005

'Sykes is a poet who is intelligent and often vivid – "...like a grounded thing / she is learning mud / as delicious and terminal" – and *Modewarre* is an astute and rewarding collection.'

—Stephen Lawrence, *Wet Ink*

ISBN 9781876756505

Wire Dancing

Commended, FAW Anne Elder Award, 2000
Commended, Mary Gilmore Award, 2000

'In poems that are at once allusive and elusive, Sykes leaps like an acrobat between past and present, mythology and history, the everyday and the exotic, from Bosnia to the circus. And dancing nimbly along the high wires of emotion and intellect, she is passionate, witty, erudite and ironic ... I urge you ... to buy and read this book so you can share ... what could be the poetry experience of the year.'

—Bev Roberts

ISBN 9781875559909

If you would like to know more about Spinifex Press, write for a free catalogue or visit our home page.

SPINIFEX PRESS
PO Box 212,
North Melbourne,
Victoria 3051, Australia
http://www.spinifexpress.com.au